Bride Song

Contents

Background

Bride Song

Bride Song

Bride Song is a series of twelve visual biblical meditations based on the Song of Songs. Each meditation stands on its own as well as being an integral part of the whole.

The framework for the series is the beautiful square pocket or pouch that the High Priest wore over his heart. On this "Breastplate" were attached twelve precious gemstones, each representing one of the twelve tribes of Israel. Thus, symbolically, the High Priest continually carried the people of Israel in his heart before the Lord. Each of the twelve meditations in "Bride Song" corresponds with one of the precious stones; this is shown in the corners of the border that surrounds each image.

As the series unfolded to me, it became apparent that the message of the Song of Songs is more than a celebration of the love between a man and a woman. The images and ideas began to cross-reference naturally across different books of the whole Bible; both Old and New Testaments, the Scriptures as a whole. and I was able to see a little more of the heart and mind of the Heavenly Bridegroom than before.

For example, in trying to understand the significance of certain characters and incidents in the story, it became clear to me that the Watchmen could represent the Church, or certain elements within it. The implications are not comfortable! This is reflected in the disturbing images of the meditations in Stanzas 7, 8 and 9. These attempt to show a time of rejection, disobedience and the resulting suffering from different points of view: an individual human being, the People of Israel, the Persecuted Church, and the Lord, the Heavenly Bridegroom. In the following meditations it brought such joy as the depth of God's mercy and covenant love brought a real sense of celebration and hope for the future!

In the letter to the Hebrews, Jesus is described as "Our Great High Priest" who has become the one complete Sacrifice, so making atonement for the sin of the world. Now 'He ever lives to make intercession for us'. No more sacrifices are needed; He completed His mission totally when He cried out from the Cross: "It is finished!" He paid the price for His Bride and made a way for reconciliation between God and man when there was none. This truth is behind the twelve precious stones of the High Priest's Breastplate and the meditations.

Stanza 1

Meditation:

"How lovely on the mountains are the feet of them that bring good news!"
Isaiah Ch 52 verses 7-10

The four Evangelists, bringers of good news, are coming to fetch the Bride to the home the Bridegroom has been preparing. They carry a Wedding Canopy or Huppa, that has been made from a Prayer Shawl or Talith.

Read John Ch 14 verses 1-4.

Jesus is preparing a home for those who choose to belong to Him. His Father's house is a house of prayer. Our prayer should be as sweet smelling incense, creating a sense of God's presence in our homes.

As they race over the winter-clad mountains, the shadow of the Huppa causes even the fields to blossom with joy!
It is night when the bearers of the wedding canopy, together with twelve other friends of the Bridegroom, travel to the Bride with great rejoicing. Night is the start of the new day in Biblical terms...and in Israel today weddings take place as soon as the first stars can be seen in the velvet sky.

Read Genesis Ch 1 verses 3-5
Matthew Ch 5 verses 14-16

The bride is dressed in the traditional wedding garments of a Yemenite; she awaits the Bridegroom's coming with hidden longing. She has made herself ready.

"The King's daughter is all glorious within: her clothing is of wrought gold..."
Psalm 45 verse 13

"Let us be glad and rejoice and give honour to Him: for the marriage of the Lamb is come and His Wife has made herself ready."

Read Revelation Ch 19 verses 7-9
Revelation Ch 21 verses 2 and 10-27

Soon, the Bride will leave the dark tents of her old home. As her thoughts turn to her beloved her heart beats faster. In her mind's eye she sees the Shepherd King. He seems to beckon her to join Him as He grazes His flock among the lilies...

Read Ezekiel Ch 34 verses 11-16
John Ch 10 verses 1-18
John Ch 21 verses 15-19

He brought me into His banqueting house & His banner over me is Love.

My Beloved is mine & I am His... He pastures His flock among the lilies.

Stanza 2

"As an apple tree among the trees of the forest
So is my Beloved among the young men.
In His shade I took great delight and sat down,
And His fruit was sweet to my taste."
Song of Songs Ch 2 verse 3

MEDITATION

Imagine you are walking in a dark pine forest somewhere in Israel. It is hot and you are thirsty. The ground under foot is dry and un-yielding. Suddenly, in a quiet, light place, you discover an apple tree...dripping with ripe, juicy fruit! Gratefully you sit down on the soft grass that grows in the cool shade and reach up for an apple. How refreshing!

The Bride dreams of her Beloved. Her hair in all its glory streams out across the dawn sky. The lovers fly high in the sky... an image borrowed from paintings by Marc Chagall, the Russian Jewish artist who was head over heels in love with his wife, Bella and celebrated this famously in a painting.
See Song of Songs Ch 2 verse 6

Around her neck the Bride wears an inscription in Hebrew. It reads: 'ANNI LE DODI VE DODI LI.'...'I am my Beloved's and He is mine.' Close to her heart is a cluster of fragrant white flowers. Their perfume reminds her of His love. The blue lines here symbolise this love: "always going between them."

The Tree stands for the Tree of Life Himself: the Messiah, the Lord Jesus. Through His death on another Tree, we now have access to eat once more of the Tree of Life.

Read Genesis Ch 3 verses 1-13 and 22-24
1 Peter Ch 2 verses 22-25

The Bride is dressed in white garments embroidered heavily with pomegranates. Traditionally, pomegranates were crushed under foot as the bride and bridegroom entered their new home, as a prayer for God's abundant blessings on their new life together.

Read Song of songs Ch 4 verses 3 and 13
Psalm 45 verses 10-17
Song of Songs Ch 4 verses 13-14
Ephesians Ch 5 verses 2 , 25-27 and 32

The Bride and the Land are one. Both belong to their Creator, the King of the Universe.

As an apple tree among the trees of the forest, so is my Beloved among the young men. With great delight I sat in His shadow, and His fruit was sweet to my taste.

Stanza 3

"Listen! My Beloved! Behold, He is coming,
Climbing on the mountains, leaping on the hills.
My Beloved responded and said to me:
Arise my darling, my beautiful one, and come along,
For behold the winter is past,
The rains are over and gone,
The flowers have already appeared in the Land."
Song of Songs Ch 2 verses 8-13

Meditation:
What winters have you experienced? When all seems cold, stark ,bare,and joy, fragrance and fruitfulness seem but things of the past. Winters of bereavement? Of loss?....or perhaps of pain, defeat, discouragement and despair?

"BUT GOD"...
He speaks through the cycle of the seasons of renewed hope.
YES! He IS coming!
And we shall be with Him one day and all our winters will melt into glorious spring! We shall see in a new way that our sufferings were 'not so hard as we thought'...

Read Song of Songs Ch 2 verses 10-13

Remember the unexpected fragrances of Spring days?...The sound of birds, the joy of the blossom-filled trees and of warmth restoring strength, hope and vitality? This picture is filled with images from the Song of Songs: figs: ripe now after their winter-long endurance on the bare branches; pomegranates: filled with blessings; and the vines in bloom that are soon to endure the vine-dresser's pruning-knife to ensure greater fruitfulness.

The white flowers symbolise all the heavily scented flowers in the Song of Songs. They are a recurring theme in the meditations. Central to all is the apple tree: speaking of the Tree of Life: her life, her Beloved.

Read John Ch 15 verses 1-14

In the land of Israel, spring falls in the month Nissan, when Passover is celebrated in remembrance of God's great deliverance from slavery in Egypt. Central to this memorial supper is the slaying, roasting and eating of the sacrificial Lamb or Pesach. Jesus is our Passover Lamb Who laid down His life for us, His enemies.

Read 1 Peter Ch 2 verses 24-25
   Exodus Ch 12

Jesus said: "I am the Resurrection and the Life. He who believes in Me will live, even though he dies; and whoever lives and believes in Me will never die!"
John Ch11 verse 25

See! The winter is past, the rains are over & gone. Flowers appear on the earth, the season of

singing has come. The fig tree puts forth its figs & the vines are in blossom . . .

Stanza 4

"O my dove, in the clefts of the rock
In the secret place of the steep pathway,
Let Me see your form, Let Me hear your voice...
For your voice is sweet
And your form is lovely."
Song of Songs Ch 2 verse 14

MEDITATION

Do we realise just how much the heavenly Bridegroom, the Lord Jesus, longs for the sight and sound of His beloved Bride?

Bridegroom: *"All beautiful you are, my darling,*
There is no flaw in you...
You have stolen My heart,
My sister, My Bride!
You have stolen My heart
With one glance of your eyes,
With one jewel of your necklace.
How delightful is your love,
My sister, My Bride!
How much more pleasing is your love than wine,
And the fragrance of your perfume than any spice

Read: Song of Songs: Ch 4 verses 7-15; Ch 6 verses 4-5 ;
    Ch 7 verse 2

Bride: *"My Beloved is mine and I am His!*
He pastures His flock among the lilies.
Until the day breaks and the shadows flee ,
Turn, my Beloved, and be like a gazelle or a
Young stag on the rugged mountains of Bether."

Read: Song of Songs Ch 2 verses 16-17

He pictures His love as a gentle rock dove, hiding high up in a cleft of the rocky mountainside.

She sees Him as a sure-footed gazelle that can leap up on the steep, dangerous crags straight to her side, with no hesitation whatsoever!

Jesus has no hesitation in His choice of you and me...and all who make up His Bride, the new Jerusalem, the Church. He is single-minded, totally.

Apparently, the reason why a gazelle can leap fearlessly from crag to crag, is that the hind legs always track exactly into the same spot as the fore legs. It is truly 'single-footed'! I have also read somewhere that to be 'single minded' is rather like the gazelle: our conscious and unconscious minds track with each other exactly too: there is no division, no hesitation. We can go straight to the mark, like Jesus.

Read: Isaiah Ch 49 verses 1-26; Psalm 40 verse 8;
    Proverbs Ch 8 verses 22-31;
    John Ch 4 verse 32-34

"As the deer pants for the water,
So my soul pants after You, O God!
You are my friend and you are my brother,
And my soul longs after you!"

"'YES, I am coming soon.'
Amen. Come Lord Jesus."
Revelation Ch 22 verse 20

Until the day breathes & the shadows flee away, turn, my Beloved, be like a gazelle or a young

stag upon the rugged mountains! O my dove, let Me see your face, let Me hear your voice!

Stanza 5

"Set me as a seal over your heart,
Like a seal on your arm.
For love is strong as death,
Jealousy is cruel as the grave;
Its flashes are flashes of fire."
Song of Songs Ch 8 verse 6

In this visual meditation I have represented the seal by a necklace ornament. It is made up of a phrase from the Song. In the Hebrew it reads: 'Anni le dodi ve dodi li." which can be translated: "I am my beloved's and my beloved is mine." It has been drawn large and is surrounded with flames of fire. There is also a study of a fig which has been cut to reveal the myriad seeds it contains. Streams of water weave around and through these two images. In the Bible, a fig tree is often used as a symbol for Israel.

MEDITATION
Find a quiet place. Then ask God to speak to you through the picture and words of this stanza.
What do these images and ideas mean to you?:

This phrase from the Song of Songs
A seal given by a man to his beloved
Flames surrounding the sign of belonging
A fig full of seeds
Streams of living water..?

The whole of Creation is God's visual aid to us. He can speak to us through anything and anyone. What is He saying to you now?
Take time now to put down on paper what these bring to mind. Some people think better in images than in words, so you might try drawing as well as using words to express your thoughts.

Read Song of Songs Ch 2 verse 16 and Ch 6 verse 3; Ch 7 verse 10 and
*   Ch 8 verse 5*
There is a progression in the relationship. Why do you think this is?
Continue adding to your meditation sheet.
Read Hebrews Ch 4 verse 9; Malachi Ch 3 verses 2-4
Record any more ideas that come to you.

Job experienced the refining fires of God's love, and in the middle of his pain was able to sing:
"I know that my Redeemer liveth, and that in the end He will stand upon the earth.
I myself shall see Him with my own eyes, I and not another. How my heart yearns within me!"
Job Ch 19 verses 25-27

"And we, who with unveiled faces all reflect the Lord's glory, are being transformed into His likeness with ever increasing glory, which comes from the Lord, Who is the Spirit."
Read 2 Corinthians Ch 3 verse 18

The progression in the Bride and Groom's relationship is about to develop. There will be pain, disobedience and darkness, yet: there is hope!...because the water of God's Spirit is always there, the scent of water that heals and restores.

Set Me as a seal over your heart, like a seal on your arm, for Love is strong

My Beloved's
and I is
Mine

"For there is hope for a tree
when it is cut down, that it will sprout again
And its shoots will not fail
Though its stump
its roots grow old in the ground and
dies in
the
dry soil,

At the scent of water it will flourish
And put forth sprigs like a plant." Job 14:7-9
"I KNOW that my Redeemer Lives!"

as death, jealousy is cruel as the grave...its flashes are flashes of fire ...

Stanza 6

"Awake, O North Wind and Come, O South Wind!
Blow upon my garden and let my fragrance be wafted abroad!"
Song of Songs Ch 4 verse 16

Thus the Bride declares the strength of her love! She even challenges the elements to test it. Somehow this reminds me of Peter at the Last Supper when he hotly declares that he would NEVER let Jesus down and that he'd even die for his friend and teacher. Within a few hours it was a different story. Following the arrest of Jesus in Gethsemane, Peter hotly declares to an inquisitive servant girl that he did NOT know Jesus, throwing in a few choice swear words for emphasis. At this point of denial, Peter realises just how weak is his love for his friend and Lord.

MEDITATION: In the Song of Songs the Bride is often sung about as if she were a lovely garden: a secret, enclosed garden filled with refreshing, fragrant trees of every description. Everywhere delightful perfumes of a whole variety of plants surprise and enrapture.
"A garden enclosed is my sister, my bride; a spring shut up, a fountain sealed. Thy plants are an orchard of pomegranates, with pleasant fruits; camphire, with spikenard...spikenard and saffron; calamus and cinnamon, with all the trees of frankincense, myrrh and aloes along with all the finest spices. You are a garden spring, a well of fresh water and streams flowing from Lebanon!"

IMAGINE that you are in this beautiful hidden haven: what do you see, smell, hear? Can you feel the warmth of the sun on your skin as it slants down through delicate fronds and leaves? do you catch hidden fragrances as you slowly move through the tall grasses? In the background can you hear the constant rippling lilt of running water from the secret fountain at the heart of the place: shimmering, shining in the play of light through the leaves on the trees? Such a place was the Garden of Eden, where our Creator walked and talked with Adam and Eve in the cool of the day.
Read Genesis Ch 1 verses 26-31; Ch 2 verses 8-25

In the visual meditation, the North and the South winds of difficulty are shown wafting the fragrances of the secret garden out into the world. They work together for good...in the end.
Think of other gardens in the Bible: Eden, Gethsemane, Paradise. What were they like and what is their significance? Then think of the Garden Tomb where Jesus was buried, near to the place where He died, nailed to a man-made tree called a Cross.
What of the tomb? First it was filled: it held the dead body of God the Son, through Whom all things were created. His body was wrapped in linen cloths, inter-leaved with spices and precious ointments: myrrh, spikenard, aloes, maybe frankincense too... weighty and entirely restricting. Then imagine: in a blast of light and thunder of earthquake, it was emptied of all but the grave cloths, so that witnesses could see for themselves and declare: "He is not here! He has risen from the dead!"

Imagine this event in This Garden if you can... The grave transformed as God the Father, through the power of the Holy Spirit (The Ruach Ha Kodesh in Hebrew; ruach translates equally as breath, wind or spirit) raises God the Son in His awesome purity from the dead. Then there are the witnesses: what did they see, think, feel, say?
What joy there must have been in this Garden on that glorious day as the power of sin and death in all Creation was seen to have been broken...for all Time! Hallelujah!
In the picture, the cup in the sky is the Cup of Redemption that Jesus gives to a broken world. Out from the Garden flows a stream which becomes a River of Life, flowing out into the desert and causing trees to spring up. Their leaves are for the healing of the nations. Amen.
Read:Ezekiel Ch 47; Zechariah Ch 14 verses 4-8;
*   Revelation Ch 22 verses 1-5*

Awake O North Wind and come O South Wind!

Blow upon my garden and let my fragrance be wafted abroad!

Stanza 7

> *"My soul failed me when he spoke.*
> *I sought him, but found him not."*
> *Song of Songs Ch 5 verse 6*

Meditation
In the Song, the writer describes two similar occasions when the bridegroom needed his bride, but she could not or would not meet him in the way that he needed her.
Read Song of Songs Ch 3 verses 1-5 and Ch 5 verses 2-3

"I slept but my heart was awake." Perhaps this was a dream? I don't know, but if it was, it turned into a nightmare. In this visual meditation the close up of the bride's face shows her as she desperately looks for her beloved. Constantly before her in her mind's eye, she replays the scenes that have been etched into her mind: The moment when she turned over in bed and delayed going to welcome him;

Then, when she finally got up and put on the precious veil he had given her: that dreadful instant of recognition that he had gone: he had left her and didn't respond to her cry for his return.

Worse followed: in the dark night, wearing his treasured gift, she searches for him and Meets the watchmen on their nightly rounds of the city. Seeing her in her distress they are not kind

They push her around, they rough her up and humiliate her.

They take away her glorious covering.

They beat her, wound her, leave her.

"I looked for Him, but did not find Him.

I called Him, but He gave me no answer.

The watchmen found me, they beat me, they bruised me,

Those watchmen on the walls!"

Song of Songs Ch 5 verse 7

Who are these watchmen? Their job was to keep and guard the city wall and warn of possible danger. They went beyond their brief here. In the Bible, God calls His people to be watchers on the walls.

Read Isaiah Ch 62 verses 6-7

The Church, too, has been given this job. Over the centuries, how well have we carried out this responsibility? In Jewish thought the word 'Christian' is readily linked with other words: Pogrom: violent outbreaks at special festivals such as Easter (poignantly shown in the wedding scene in "Fiddler on the Roof";) Inquisition: leading to forced conversion, torture or exile; and in this century, the Holocaust.

As I worked on this meditation, it came to me that the bride can be seen in several ways: a young girl in love, a person seeking to know God, or the Jewish people or the Church. How do you think the situation will be resolved for the Bride? On a human and spiritual level, she has some problems to deal with in the relationship. She has left her first love.

If I was thinking of her as a follower of Jesus, then maybe she has been putting off that time alone with Him, letting someone or something get in the way; or maybe she did not recognise Jesus when He came to her as a needy friend, or stranger, or enemy, and the sense of His presence evaporated.

When thinking of her as Israel or the Church, time and again in the scriptures God speaks of His people as a bride, entering into a covenant relationship that is eternal. He re-affirms this in **Jeremiah Ch 31 and Ezekiel Ch 36**. He has not divorced the Jewish people or the Church; He longs for all to return to His side: freely and for love. When we turn away from Him, He cannot make us love Him, but longs for our love with incomprehensible depths of yearning, and will do what is necessary to draw us back to Himself.

> **"Therefore I am now going to allure her;**
> **I will lead her into the desert**
> **And speak tenderly to her.**
> **In that day, declares the Lord,**
> **You will call Me 'My Husband', 'Ishi'.**
> **You will no longer call Me 'My Master': 'Baali'.**
> **Hosea Ch 2 verses 14-23**

I slept but my heart was awake··· I opened to my Beloved but my Beloved had turned

and gone. My soul failed me when He spoke. I sought Him, but found Him not, I called Him ···

Stanza 8

"The watchmen found me
They beat me;
They wounded me;
They took away my mantle."
Song of Songs Ch 5 verses 6-7

MEDITATION

> *"At least there is hope for a tree:*
> *If it is cut down it will sprout again,*
> *And its new shoots will not fail.*
> *Its roots may grow old in the ground*
> *And its stump die in the soil,*
> *Yet at the scent of water it will bud*
> *And put forth shoots like a plant."*
> *Job Ch 14 verses 7-9*

The tree and the woman represent the Bride. They could be you or me, they are also symbols of the Land of Israel: cut off from God and yet longing for Him with a nameless longing in her blindness. "He" is the Bridegroom: the Shepherd-Messiah.
Read Romans Ch 11 verses 17-23

She reaches out... like the arms of the holocaust victims in a monument at the Yad Va Shem. In despair, yet still reaching out for Him in the dark tunnel of suffering: fear, exile, loss, rejection, death... Auschwitz, Belsen...
Read Hosea Ch2 verses 14-23

Her eyes yearn for the light and for hope; she feels abandoned by all in whom she had put her trust. Yet all the time the Bridegroom Himself is drawing her back home to His arms, through the dread tunnel of suffering...to a garden and the right to eat fruit from the Tree of Life. The Redeemer King is near.

The Messiah Himself is The Door to this place of safety at the end of the tunnel. Through Him is the place of safety, hope, protection and redemption. The bride may freely eat of the Tree of Life...no longer rejected and locked outside.

The shadow of the cross marks the beginning of the tunnel, but its shadow casts light rather than darkness. Jesus is the only way through it. Blue lines representing the Holy Spirit, reach out from the Bridegroom and though unrecognised, are working to draw her through to safety.

The garden and all that it represents will be restored to all who will go through the Door; there is only this Door. It is small and humble, no bigger than a Man dying on a man-made tree.

Jesus of Nazareth, Son of David and Son of God, says:
"I AM the door; whoever enters by Me will be saved."

Read John Ch10 verse 9 and John Ch 14, verses 1-6

...but He gave me no answer...The watchmen found me. They beat me, they wounded me

they took away my veil, the guardsmen on the wall ...

Stanza 9

"How is your beloved better than others, most beautiful of women?"
"My beloved is radiant and ruddy, outstanding among ten thousand.
His head is gold, pure gold. He is altogether lovely.
This is my lover, this my friend, O daughters of Jerusalem."
Song of Songs Ch 5 verses 9-16

Questions rather than answers are more frequently our salvation than we realise. At least that was my experience: at art college following yet another discussion (during a break for the life model to rest), a friend asked me: " Christine, what are you really looking for?" The question triggered an amazing reaction. It would not leave me till I'd thought it through. In our next class, realising what my answer was, I walked over to Cameron (the wiser, older member of our group) and blurted out, rather tearfully: "I know what I'm looking for: I'm looking for the Truth: I just want to know what's real. That's all."

For the despairing bride, a well-timed question from close observers provokes a heart-felt response. She stops to think about just who it is that she is looking for. Her mind is flooded with all that she knows him to be...and she can't stop talking about him!
It struck me that as soon as the focus was back on HIM and away from her sin and failure and pain,...then He was back!

MEDITATION: *"His head was gold, pure gold."*
In the Hebrew, two different words are used for gold: the first is **Kethem**, which is pure gold, the second is **Paz** which is fine gold.
Gold: precious, pure, fine, shining. Able to withstand the highest temperatures in a furnace, it can be stretched out into the finest thread that will not break when stretched to the uttermost. When it is fully refined and still liquid, gold perfectly reflects the image of its refiner as he bends over to check if his work is complete.

Read:Hebrews Ch 1 verse 2;
Colossians Ch 1 verses 15-20;
Song of Songs Ch 5 verses 9-16
Read through the above passages slowly, after asking God to reveal something of His glory to you.
After reading through at least twice, reflect on the words relating to "gold" and "pure".
Be silent before the Lord for a while. Then begin to praise Him for Who He is.
Read Song of Songs Ch 8 verse 7

This picture shows the same situation as in Stanzas 7 and 8, but from Heaven's perspective. The King, who is also the Shepherd and the Bridegroom, steadfastly keeps the vision of their Garden relationship restored. The oil of God's anointing power is poured out on his head. In the heavens we see His Spirit: the blue swirling lines, battling to defeat the waves and billows of the enemy of the Truth.

The Shepherd will not fail. He is the Victor. Steadfastly He looks to the completion of the task. He will pay the complete Redemption price for His Bride and take the full force of God's wrath against sin, in His own body on a Tree.

Read: Hebrews Ch 12 verses 1-2 and 1 Peter Ch 1 verses 7 and 13-21

What is your Beloved more than another beloved? He is the fairest among ten thousand

His head is gold, pure gold. He is altogether desirable. This is my Beloved & this my friend.

Stanza 10

"Where has your beloved gone,
O, most beautiful of women...
That we may seek him with you?"
"My beloved has gone down to his garden,
To the beds of spices, to feed in the gardens,
And to gather lilies; I am my beloved's and he is mine."
Song of Songs Ch 6 verses 1-3

MEDITATION

In my mind's eye I can see the shepherd as he strides down the hillside through the rich pasture to the garden. I have seen fields like this and painted them one Spring on the mountains of Naphtali, opposite the Mount Hermon range in Upper Galilee. The rich green fields are woven with glorious flowers of every hue, but in particular, the great blood red anemones, like jewels set in green.

Carried high on his shoulder, the shepherd bears a lamb...tenderly, carefully, as he hastens to share the good news of the rescue! The 'found' sheep will spend time recovering and resting close to the Rescuer's heart. The shepherd will deliberately make sure that this happens, and will do whatever is necessary to ensure the creature's ultimate safety. Thus the sheep develops such a deep relationship of trust and love with its owner, that now, of its own free will it will always choose to stay close by his side.

Read Luke Ch 15 verses 3-7

The joy of restoration is the key to this visual biblical meditation The garden is almost bursting out of the picture and the fragrances mingle and swirl out into the firmament... The Cup runs over while the light of the sun and moon are eclipsed by the brightness of this glory!

The Garden represents the Bride. Reconciliation makes its beauty even more radiant. The cup of the bitterness of separation and death has become the Cup of Redemption. The fragrance of the Shepherd King's sacrificial "agape" love fills the world, the universe.

Read 2 Corinthians Ch 2 verse 14
Hebrews Ch 10 verses 5-9

The bridegroom sings of His Beloved's beauty.
He has no thoughts of condemnation.
Joy fills His being.

Read Song of Songs Ch 6 verses 4-10
Romans Ch 8 verses 1-2, 31-39
Luke Ch 23 verse 34
John Ch 10 verses 11-18

My Beloved has gone down to His garden, to pasture His flock in the gardens, & gather lilies. I am my Beloved's and my Beloved is mine. He who pastures His flocks among the lilies.

Song

gardens and gather lilies. I am my Beloved's and my Beloved is mine.

Stanza 11

> *"Love is strong as death. Its flashes are flashes of fire.*
> *Many waters cannot quench love, neither can floods drown it!"*
> *Song of Songs Ch 8 verse 7*

MEDITATION

It is hard to realise just how strong and faithful is this love in the Song until we look at the lengths and depths that God went to for His Creation. This is not a sentimental, cosy kind of love. It is true, and real and pure. The Lord also has demands of us: that we too are faithful...unto death...

When completing this visual meditation, I realised the significance of the wounds that Messiah Jesus sustained on our behalf. His motive was always love: that sacrificial agape love that led Him to lay down His life for His friends...and His enemies, calling on His Father to forgive them, "for they don't know what they are doing."

At first, when designing this stanza, I indicated five wounds, those touches of red in and amongst the waves of darkness and destruction. Then I realised the were six wounds: to His head, to both hands and feet, and His heart: His heart that broke with the pain of becoming sin for us and suffering separation from His Father for the first time...beyond time. Later, His heart was thrust through with a spear, then blood and water flowed out: this was clear proof of death. The Resurrection was truly life from the dead.

As I meditated on this, I saw the significance of the number six. Mankind was created on Day Six (Yom Shishi in the Hebrew) Jesus, the last Adam, was crucified on the sixth day

Six is the number that symbolises mankind and incompletion. Seven is the number of completion, of rest. On Day Seven (Yom Shabbat) the Lord God rested from all His work. Jesus' love for His Father enabled Him to complete the work of Redemption, of buying back the lost creation. His last triumphant cry from the Cross was: "Tetelestai!" "It is finished!" "It is completed!"

As a result of spending time in the Song of Songs I have gained a greater understanding of the depth of God's mercy and love for me and the whole of His Creation.

We probably will never be able to comprehend the significance of every detail of God's rescue plan for us all, but it matters to realise that you too are a significant part of this plan, that He knows you by name and longs for you to walk and talk with Him in the cool of the day...
Read Genesis Ch1 verses 24-31 and Genesis Ch 2 verses 1-2
> *Matthew Ch 27 verses 27-46*
> *Luke Ch 23 verses 26-46*
> *John Ch 19 verses 28-37*
> *1 Corinthians Ch 15 verses 20-23, 45-58*

"Death has been swallowed up in victory!" "Where, O Death, is your sting?" "The sting of Death is sin, and the power of sin is the Law. But...thanks be to God! He gives us the victory through our Lord Jesus Christ!"
1 Corinthians Ch 15 verses 54-58 Isaiah Ch 25 verses 6-9

Love is strong as death, its flashes are flashes of fire. Many waters cannot

quench Love, neither can floods drown it! I am my Beloved's and He is for me!

Stanza 12

"Who is this that cometh up from the Wilderness,
Leaning upon her beloved?"
Song of Songs Ch 8 verse 5

In this visual meditation we see the human side of the reconciliation between shepherd and sheep portrayed in Stanza 10. The couple walk together, climbing the steep ascent up from the Dead Sea and out of the Wilderness. They wear crowns of flowers, like those they had on their wedding day, when they first made their vows to each other. His right arm embraces her; he covers her with his outer garment. This is another covenant sign of protection and shelter.

Read Isaiah Ch 61 verses10-Ch 62 verse 4
    Ruth Ch 3 verses 4-9
So now she clings to him, knowing her own weakness and the steadfastness of his love for her. She is still in shock at the realisation of how she could so easily have left her first love.

The Shepherd-King-Bridegroom grasps His staff of authority and a sprig of myrtle. There is a reason for this image, of course! Some years ago when reading Isaiah Ch 55 I questioned the reason for myrtle growing instead of nettles. So began a search that lead to some special discoveries.

I began to realise that myrtle is a hidden symbol for the Messiah. It is a humble shrub with amazing properties. It has a woody stem, full of aromatic oils. If you crush a stem or leaf in your hands it gives out a refreshing fragrance. It has healing properties, is antiseptic and produces delicate creamy white flowers, then purplish berries that can be eaten. If a myrtle tree is burnt, then it will grow back again, this time with three leaf nodes instead of two. Myrtle is symbolic of humility, healing, immortality and success; traditionally it is used at weddings and funerals. Nettles and thistles only hurt back.
Read Isaiah Ch 55 verse 13

The bridegroom's face is quiet. He knows that the bridal Redemption price is His own life.
Read Isaiah Ch 53
"He was pierced for our transgressions, He was crushed for our iniquity,...The Lord has laid on Him the iniquity of us all."
To the left of the picture, up in the sky, is the future Wedding Feast of the Lamb and His Bride. They are at the beginning of the new Heaven and the new Earth.
"The voice of joy and the voice of rejoicing, the voice of the bride and the voice of the Bridegroom!"
Read Revelation Ch 21 verses 1-3 & Jeremiah Ch 33 verse 11
The Bride wears her veil. Initially she was drawn without the rather strange middle-eastern covering and her hair flowed free, but I felt very uncomfortable about this. Peace returned to my heart as soon as the veil was included. I realised that the veil was a picture of the anointing of the Holy Spirit and symbolic of her undivided heart. At last she has single-hearted trust in her Husband!
Read Ezekiel Ch 47 verses 1-12
    Revelation Ch 22 verses 1-5
    Jeremiah Ch 17 verses 7-8
Now the River of Life flows out into the Dead Sea. The healing of its salt laden waters takes place at last and fish can be seen coming and going from its once lifeless depths. On either side of the River are trees whose leaves are for the healing of the nations. What are they, these trees? Are they people: living letters? Or something entirely different? I'm still thinking about that. What is sure is that Jesus' triumphant shout is this:
"Behold, I make all things new!"
Read Revelation Ch 21 verses 3-5
With Him, one day there will be no more tears, no more sorrow nor crying nor pain; and no more death, for the former things have passed away. AMEN."

Who is this coming up from the Wilderness leaning upon her Beloved?

He was pierced through for our rebellion. The chastening for our well-being fell upon Him. Isaiah 53 v 5

THE HIGH PRIEST'S BREASTPLATE
Exodus Ch 28 and Hebrews Ch 4 verse14 ...

The Breastplate was worn only by the High Priest. He wore it as a representative of the people of Israel before Almighty God, the Holy One. It was an extremely beautiful pocket or pouch worn over the heart and it was also an integral part of the ephod. The ephod was a sleeveless ceremonial over-garment worn over the blue robe and the white tunic made from fine twined linen.

The Breastplate was a span square (about nine inches) a span being the distance between the tip of the thumb and the tip of the little finger. It was made from the same materials the ephod: "gold and blue and purple and scarlet and fine twined linen". Twelve precious stones were set in gold filigree on the front in four rows of three. Upon each stone was engraved the name of a tribe of Israel "in order of their tribes". The pouch contained the Urim and Thummim which were used to determine God's will concerning individuals and the People of Israel. That is why it is referred to as the "Breastplate of Judgement".

Four gold rings, one attached to each corner, were used to fasten the breastplate to the ephod: the top two linked by twisted gold cords or chains to engraved onyx stones set in gold, one on each shoulder; the bottom two corners were joined to two or more gold rings at the sides, one on either edge of the ephod and just above the intricately woven sash or girdle that held everything in place. On the onyx shoulder stones were engraved the names of the twelve tribes, six on each shoulder, this time in their birth order.

Thus, symbolically, the High Priest was to bear the people on his shoulders and carry them in his heart before the Holy One, the Creator of all things, as he made intercession and performed the sacrifices. He is a picture of the Lord Jesus (Yeshuah in Hebrew), who became the complete sacrifice, was acceptable to His Father, and raised from the dead because of His perfect, obedient and sinless life. According to the writer of the letter to the Hebrews, He now lives to make intercession for us at the Father's right hand on high.

"The High Priest's Breastplate"
Exodus 28

The Precious Stones in Exodus 28

Please note:
As Hebrew is written from right to left, the stones would have been set in the same way.
According to research, the exact translation to corresponding stones today is not always possible. See Appendix 2 for more detailed information. I am indebted to the book "Gems Tell Their Secret" for all the following.

The first row:	**BARAKETH**	**PITADEH**	**ODEM**
	green	yellow	red
	emerald	topaz	ruby
	3	2	1

The second row:	**YAHALOM**	**SAPPIR**	**NOPHEK**
	clear	blue	red
	diamond	sapphire	garnet
	6	5	4

The third row:	**ACHLEMAH**	**SHEBU**	**LESHEM**
	purple	yellow	multiple
	amethyst	agate	opal
	9	8	7

The fourth row:	**YASHAPHEH**	**SHOHAM**	**TARSHISH**
	black & red	black & brown	turquoise
	jasper	sardonyx	turquoise
	12	11	10

SONNET CXVI

"Let me not to the marriage of true minds
Admit impediments. Love is not love which alters
When it alteration finds
Or bends with the remover to remove.
Oh no! it is an ever fixed mark
That looks on tempests and is never shaken.
It is the star to every wandering bark
Who's worth's unknown 'though its height be taken.
Love's not time's fool, though rosy lips and cheeks
Within his bending sickle's compass comes.
Love alters not with his brief hours and weeks,
But bears it out even to the edge of doom.
If this be false and upon me proved,
I never writ nor no man ever loved."
William Shakespeare

THE PRECIOUS STONES: details

Source: "Gems Tell Their Secret"

Odem/Ruby   This stone has many impurities. Its colour is hard to describe, the nearest comparison is pigeon's blood.

Pitadeh/Topaz   Golden yellow and clear, "pitadeh" means "The Yellow One". Shipwrecked sailors once landed on an island in the Red Sea and found the stone there. Both the island and the stone they named "Topazos" ie 'lost and found'.

Bereketh/Emerald   Its many inclusions can make it seem as if it contains a miniaturised garden. It is rarely pure. Symbol of new life and hope.

Nophek/Garnet   Called "little coal" because of its deep glowing red colour. Its beauty with its transparency.

Sappir/Sapphire   Same chemical composition as a ruby. Traces of iron and titanium cause the blue colour. It is possible that in the Old Testament the word sappir stands for lapis lazuli, a deep, blue stone, flecked with traces of fool's gold, like stars in the evening sky. In my representation of the Breastplate, both ideas are shown. (Job Ch 28 verse 6)

Yahalom/Diamond   Formed from black dust (carbon) under extreme pressure. Its tremendous hardness, refractivity and sparkling fire fascinate again and again. It is the only gem containing a single element. Cutting in the hands of an expert releases the fire.

Leshem/Opal   Iridescent phenomenon: a rainbow-like play of colours that alters according to the point of view. Mysterious, containing a soft fire aglow with all the colours of the other gemstones. (2 Corinthians Ch 9 verse 15)

Shebu/Agate   Rich variation of colours formed by rhythmic crystalisation. Found inside geodes: volcanic rock. When split open the treasure is revealed: bands of yellow, grey, brown, always in surprising harmony.

Achlemah/Amethyst   Purple to dark violet; clear. Royal colour, central strand of the three colours of the High Priest's over garment. (Called the ephod, it includes the Breastplate: blue and purple and scarlet, pure white linen and gold thread woven together intricately.)

Tarshish/Turquoise   One of the few gems not created by high heat or pressure, but through the slow seepage of water through the rocks. Found in the Sinai desert. Turquoise from this area has the quality of precious stones. the most common colour is blue-green.

Shoham/Onyx   The sardonyx has white layers alternated with brown ones. The onyx has a white top layer combined with a black bottom one. Parallel bands of light and dark layers. The skilled stone cutter can create a thing of beauty from darkness and light. Onyx is Greek for fingernail because of its translucent character. Not transparently clear, but almost!

Yashapheh/Jasper   Iron-quartz or jasper belongs to the opaque and impure quartz varieties. Mostly yellow, brown or red, sometimes variegated or even banded. In the New testament the jasper of Revelation 21 v 11 is described as having diamond like qualities: clear, transparent and precious. In my representation of the High Prist's Breastplate, both ideas are shown. One could symbolise the earthly High Preist and the other, the diamond, Jesus: the one, true Great High Priest of the order of Melchizedek, who ever lives to make intercession for us: King, Priest and Sacrifice.

THE PRECIOUS STONES: various translations:

Hebrew	Septuagint Greek translation (c. 200 BC)	King James Version	New Translation JN Darby
Odem	Sardion	Sardius	Sardion
Pitadeh	Topazion	Topaz	Topaz
Bareketh	Smaragdos	Carbuncle	Emerald
Nophek	Antrax	Emerald	Carbuncle
Sappir	Sappheiros	Sapphire	Sapphire
Yahalom	Iaspis	Diamond	Diamond
Leshem	Ligurion	Ligure	Opal
Shebu	Achates	Agate	Agate
Tarshish	Chrusolithos	Beryl	Chrysolite
Shoham	Berullos	Onyx	Onyx
Yashapheh	Onuchion	Jasper	Jasper

The Bride Price

There was once a man, it has been told, who lived on a small island community of about two hundred souls, somewhere in the South Pacific. He was a sharp kind of guy (It was an American telling the story), a bit of an entrepreneur, and always good at getting a bargain. He became wealthy and was looked up to by many of the islanders. He drove a hard bargain time after time until he became even more wealthy and more respected.

The time came for him to seek a bride and the islanders were agog with curiosity to see who he would choose: surely some beautiful, high class girl. But no, his choice was a poor farmer's daughter, homely, nothing special to look at. Kind, but quiet and ordinary.

Now the custom was for the future son-in-law to pay a bride-price to the father: in cows. So a two or three bride-price was quite special. The islanders were again agog (there being not too much to gossip about in the small community) to see how many cows he would pay for his bride, especially when they considered his bargaining skills.

Can you guess how many? They were all totally amazed to see him take no less than seven cows to his future father-in-law...who was himself not a little surprised: he'd never thought her much of a catch and was relieved to have her off his hands.

A year later it was a different story. The new bride was transformed; her beauty now shone. She was a calm, confident woman of grace, almost like a princess in the way she lived and carried herself. On a rare visit to celebrate the first anniversary, the father saw the difference and complained to his son-in-law:
"You only gave me seven cows for this radiant beauty, my daughter! Give me more; you have cheated me!"

His son-n-law merely smiled and said,
"No. What you have not done for her all her life, my love has accomplished for her in one year."

The reporter to whom this story was being recounted had a burning question:
"Why did you actually give seven cows for her? You could have got her for less and still have made an honourable transaction."

The wise husband replied:
"Ah, but you see, I wanted a seven cow bride, and see, I got what I paid for."

The husband knew the secret of his young bride's transformation: honour.
He loved, honoured and esteemed her. She became what he saw in her.

BRIDAL VERSES

Isaiah 61 v 10-11

"I will rejoice greatly in the LORD,
My soul will exult in my God;
For He has clothed me with the garments of salvation,
He has wrapped me with a robe of righteousness,
As a bridegroom decks himself with a garland,
And as a bride adorns herself with her jewels.
For as the earth brings forth its sprouts,
And as a garden causes the things sown in it to spring up,
So the LORD God will cause righteousness and praise
To spring up before all nations."

Isaiah 62 v 1-5

"For Zion's sake I will not keep silent,
And for Jerusalem's sake I will not keep quiet,
Until her righteousness goes forth like brightness,
And her salvation like a torch that is burning,
And the nations will see your righteousness,
And all kings your glory;
And you will be called by a new name,
Which the mouth of the LORD will designate."
"You will also be a crown of beauty in the hand of the LORD ,
And a royal diadem in the hand of your God.
It will no longer be said of you: "Forsaken,"
Nor to your land will it any more be said, "Desolate;"

But you will be called "Hephzibah" (My delight is in her")
And your land "Beulah" (Married;")
For as a young man marries a virgin, so your sons will marry you;
And as a bridegroom rejoices over the bride,
So your God will rekoice over you."

Revelation 19 v 7-9

'"Let us rejoice and be glad and give the glory to Him, for the marriage of
the Lamb has come and His bride has made herself ready."
And it was given to her to clothe herself in fine linen, bright and clean,
For the fine linen is the righteous deeds of the saints.'

Revelation 21 v 9 ff

'"Come here, I shall show you the Bride, the wife of the Lamb."
And he carried me away in the Spirit to a great and high mountain, and
showed me the holy city, Jerusalem, coming down out of heaven from God,
having the glory of God.
Her brilliance was like a very costly stone, as a stone of crystal clear jasper.
It had a great and high wall, with twelve gates, and at the gates twelve
angels; and the names were written on them which are those of the twelve
tribes of the sons of Israel. There were three gates on the east and three
gates on the north and three gates on the south and three gates on the west.
And the wall of the city had twelve foundation stones, and on them were
the twelve names of the twelve apostles of the Lamb.'

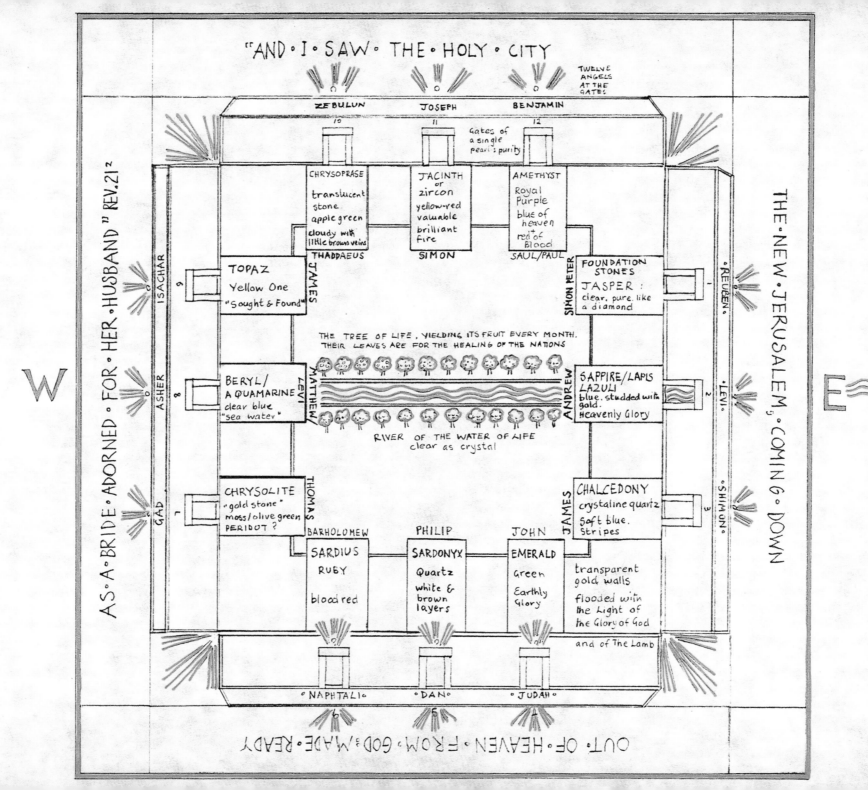

Explanation:

Although impossible to imagine, the Heavenly City is fifteen hundred miles cubed. Enormous! Astronomically so! Room for all. Its walls are seventy-two yards thick, so it is absolutely safe from all harm. "And the material of the wall was jasper, and the city was pure gold, like clear glass." As the Apostle John looked up at this marvel, the whole place must have shone and sparkled against the beautiful blue heavens.

The four square shape in three dimensions speaks of the perfection of the city. The shining transparency speaks of the light and the absolute truth of this place. Nothing is hidden; all is revealed and transfigured by the Light of the World, the Lamb of God.

Nothing belonging to darkness can enter here: no tears, mourning, pain or death; no cowards, immoral; nothing unclean. Only those who have come to the Lamb to be washed clean and made new, whose names have been written in the Lamb's book of Life can enter. And enter they will, from every tribe and tongue and nation, coming to bring their glory and honour to Him as joyful tribute. Let us make sure that each of us is inscribed in the Lamb's Book of Life. No other book will do. Then we too, like the bride in the Song of Songs, will have made ourselves ready for the Heavenly Bridegroom, King of Kings and Lord of Lords and Prince of Peace.

I found it difficult to draw the heavenly city in real terms, so I did the next best thing and tried to see it through the eyes of a child. So the three dimensional cube has become a square, like the High Priest's Breastplate. There are other similarities to the Breastplate which I hope the reader will have seen: the twelve tribes, the twelve precious stones, the shining glory and beauty of it all. Differences there are, the twelve apostles of the Lamb and the size being the most obvious. However, the twelve tribes of Israel remain, the apostles are all Jewish, as is the Lamb, Messiah Jesus, our Great High Priest. The borders of blue represent the blue heavens, sprinkled with stars, and reminds me of the blue robe worn by the High Priest under the ephod. The city walls have a chequered effect, to remind us of the linen tunic made of fine twisted linen, in a damask type woven pattern. The bride was dressed in this type of fine linen, "which is the righteous deeds of the saints'. Revelation Ch 19 v 7-8

The city, seen descending from the heavens, is brilliant with glorious light: transparent, crystal-clear jasper, like a diamond rather than the natural form of jasper, which is a dull, opaque stone, grey and speckled with red. Such is the difference between the first and the last man Adam. (See 1 Corinthians Ch15 v 45) Its walls are very thick and very high, so it is safe from all harm and nothing that is not made clean and bright by the Lamb of God can enter that place. The gates by which people may enter are very different: each is made from a single pearl. Such a strange image! What could it mean? I quote from "Gems Tell Their Secret":

"Pearls speak of purity. A pearl begins with something ugly or worthless, like a grain of sand or dirt. It finds its way into the oyster and becomes gradually surrounded with mother of pearl: clothed with beauty and iridescent splendour. A pearl is an image of purity. It speaks of the Church, of the bride bought by Christ, of her value to Him and of how His heart rejoices, because He has purchased her as His precious bride. "

So we have now come full circle: from the love of God for a particular people shown through His loving discipline of them in the Wilderness years, symbolised by the High Priest's Breatplate of Judgement, to a love song at the heart of the scriptures called the Song of Songs, and on to the end of time as we know it when the heavenly city, in all its stunning purity and beauty is seen descending from heaven "as a bride adorned for her husband." As you, dear reader, share some of the things given to me, may they encourage you to believe that what God has started, so He will finish.. What he created in the beginning was good, very good. What it will be in the end will also be good, very good.

"Maranatha!
Even so, come Lord Jesus. Amen!"

The Heavenly City
Adorned like a bride for her husband

Read Revelations Ch 21 verse 2-Ch 22 verse 5

"And I saw the holy city, the New Jerusalem, coming down out of heaven from God, made ready as a bride adorned for her husband. And I heard a loud voice from the throne, saying, "Behold, the tabernacle of God is among men, and He shall dwell among them and they shall be His people, and God Himself shall wipe away every tear from their eyes; and there shall no longer be any death; there shall no longer be any mourning, or crying, or pain; the first things have passed away."

"And one of the seven angels...came and spoke with me, saying, "Come here and I will show you the bride, the wife of the Lamb." And he carried me away and showed me the holy city, Jerusalem, coming down out of heaven from God, having the glory of God.
Her brilliance was like a very costly stone, as a stone of crystal clear jasper. It had a great high wall, with twelve gates, and at the gates twelve angels; and names were written on them, which are those of the twelve tribes of the sons of Israel. There were three gates on the east and three gates on the north and three gates on the south and three gates on the west. And the wall of the city had twelve foundation stones, and on them were the twelve names of the twelve apostles of the Lamb.

"And the one who spoke with me had a golden measuring rod to measure the city, and its gates and its wall. And the city was laid out as a square, and its length is as great as its width; and he measured the city with his rod, fifteen hundred miles (twelve thousand stadia); its length and width and height are equal. And he measured its wall, seventy two yards (a hundred and forty four cubits)...and the material of the wall was jasper and the city was pure gold, like clear glass. The foundation stones of the city were adorned with every kind of precious stone.

The first foundation was jasper; the second, sapphire; the third, chalcedony;
      the fourth, emerald; the fifth, sardonyx; the sixth, sardius;
      the seventh, chrysolite; the eighth, beryl; the ninth, topaz;
      the tenth, chrysoprase; the eleventh, jacinth; the twelfth, amethyst.

And the twelve gates were twelve pearls; each one of the gates was a single pearl. And the street of the city was pure gold, like transparent glass. And I saw no temple in it, for the LORD God, the Almighty, and the Lamb, are its temple. And the city has no need of sun or moon to shine upon it, for the glory of God has illumined it, and its lamp is the Lamb..."

"And he showed me a river of the water of life, clear as crystal, coming from the throne of God and of the Lamb, in the middle of its street. And on either side of the river was the tree of life, bearing twelve kinds of fruit, yielding its fruit every month; and the leaves of the tree were for the healing of the nations."

Post Script

The Bride Song project began back in the late 1980s when two friends in Israel, Etti and Janne, invited me to look at the Song of Songs and come up with some drawings suitable for use in the construction and decoration of a Messianic Wedding Canopy or Huppa for use in the congregation there in Tel Aviv.

So I began in an old green exercise book with reading through and noting down scents and sounds and images. Very soon I gave that up and started sketching in my blue biro (can't rub this out!) and adding colour rapidly as the images began to flow, rather like those in a classic film poster. The first was Stanza 4, about the dove and the deer. It was clear from the start that they should become a book, perhaps with a fold down the middle. This is apparent in the design of each visual meditation or stanza. Another friend, Liz Dale, gave me the booklet, 'Gems Tell Their Secret' which added enormously relevant information. Then it was friends Dan and Henrijka who encouraged me to start refining these for exhibiting at a Messianic Conference back in 1991. Over the next decade the book came together with its borders and meditations, almost as a 'gift'.
Incorporated into the images are the sights and sounds experienced through several periods in the Land of Israel including a long period, working with an international team on two kibbutzim, both having splendid views of beautiful Mount Hermon.

Under-pinning all of the above has to be a love of the Word of God and the Scriptures. My thanks go out to all who introduced me early to the biblical practice of meditating in scripture, especially Ruth Giesner, Alex Buchanan, Denis Clark and Ken and Lillie Burnett... and many others on the way. These scribbles and thoughts are part of the process of learning to listen to the Lord in a way that was relevant to me. They are what they are and are offered here as this booklet for any who, like me, were/are searching after something they can't see or grasp but feel such a longing for that they have no rest or peace in their innermost beings until they find it out.

As a young art student, that was my story. My search was for reality, for the truth. My discovery is the secret hidden in the Song of Songs and through all Scripture, from Genesis to Revelation: that reality is another word for truth and that the truth is a person: Jesus the Messiah, Son of God, Saviour. When at a key and low point in my life, an art technician (who was a very new believer in Jesus) jokingly said: "Seek and you will find" about something and the conversation turned immediately to Jesus. Soon after this I was offered a book to read: 'Man Alive' by Michael Green. It was about the evidence for Jesus' Resurrection and answered many questions I had about this very issue. It was like a veil taken off my eyes and I saw the truth and welcomed Him! There was immense joy in this discovery. This new believer and his dear wife became true friends. So thank you both, Simon and Maggie and all others who prayed me into the Kingdom in those dark and searching days, and led me out into His light and life.

My hope is that this collection of pictures and meditations will bless and encourage all who are searching for that missing something: in whatever area of life! May you be found by the Good Shepherd Himself! Amen.

Acknowledgements:
I have mostly used the New American Standard Bible, with some quotes from the Authorised Version and the New International Versions of the Bible.
I am indebted to the booklet 'Gems Tell Their Secret' by J. Rowe available through www.chaptertwobooks.org.uk
The story of the Bride Price was heard a long time ago at a teaching seminar given by a visiting speaker at my church in North London, and seemed to fit in to the series. Thank you, who ever you are!
I have to add my thanks to Hazel and Robert Blayney – my Art teacher and husband, for their encouragement over the years – Christine Maybank.
Shavuot/Pentecost 2011 SDG.